Pebble™ Plus

A Visit to

The Supermarket

by B. A. Hoena

Consulting Editor: Gail Saunders-Smith, Ph.D.
Reading Consultant: Jennifer Norford, Senior Consultant
Mid-continent Research for Education and Learning
Aurora, Colorado

Capstone press

Mankato, Minnesota

Pebble Plus is published by Capstone Press
151 Good Counsel Drive, P.O. Box 669, Mankato, Minnesota 56002
www.capstonepress.com

1 2 3 4 5 6 09 08 07 06 05 04

Library of Congress Cataloging-in-Publication Data
Hoena, B. A.
The supermarket/by B. A. Hoena.
p. cm.—(Pebble plus, A visit to)
Includes bibliographical references and index.
Contents: The supermarket—Departments—Checking out.
ISBN 0-7368-2393-X (hardcover)
1. Supermarkets—Juvenile literature. [1. Supermarkets. 2. Grocery shopping.] I. Title. II. Series.
HF5469.H59 2004
381'.456413—dc22   2003011994

Editorial Credits

Sarah L. Schuette, editor; Jennifer Bergstrom, series designer; Karen Risch, product planning editor

Photo Credits

Capstone Press/Gary Sundermeyer, front cover, 1, 4–5, 7, 8–9, 11, 12–13, 14–15, 17, 18–19, 20–21
PhotoDisc Inc., back cover

The publisher does not endorse products whose logos may appear on objects in images in this book.

Note to Parents and Teachers

The series A Visit to supports national social studies standards related to the production, distribution, and consumption of goods and services. This book describes and illustrates a visit to a supermarket. The images support early readers in understanding the text. The repetition of words and phrases helps early readers learn new words. This book also introduces early readers to subject-specific vocabulary words, which are defined in the Glossary section. Early readers may need assistance to read some words and to use the Table of Contents, Glossary, Read More, Internet Sites, and Index/Word List sections of the book.

Word Count: 123
Early-Intervention Level: 14

Table of Contents

The Supermarket

A supermarket is a busy place to visit. Shoppers buy groceries at a supermarket.

Shoppers use carts or baskets. They push the carts through the store. They carry baskets.

Shoppers look up and down aisles. They find the items on their shopping lists.

Departments

The produce department
is large. Shoppers pick out
fresh fruits and vegetables.

The deli has meats,
cheeses, and salads.
Some deli workers slice
meat to make sandwiches.

The bakery has cakes,
breads, and cookies.
Bakery workers
frost cakes.

Some workers stock
the shelves. They fill the
shelves with cans, boxes,
and packages.

The Checkout

Cashiers work at checkout lines. They tell shoppers the cost of their groceries.

19

A supermarket is
an important place.
People buy the food they
need at a supermarket.

Glossary

aisle—the area in a supermarket that runs between two rows of shelves; most aisles have signs that list the items that can be found there.

bakery—a place where workers bake breads, cakes, and other foods in large ovens

cashier—a person who adds up grocery bills, takes money from shoppers, and gives change back to shoppers

deli—a store or place that sells food that is ready to eat; shoppers can buy sandwiches, salads, and hot foods in the deli of a supermarket.

groceries—the items that people buy; shoppers buy milk, bread, and many other groceries at a supermarket.

produce—the items that people grow for eating; fruits and vegetables are produce items; many supermarkets have large produce sections.

Read More

Canizares, Susan. *Supermarket.* Scholastic Placebook. New York: Scholastic, 2002.

Gallacher, Lorraine. *Let's Go to the Supermarket!* New York: Simon Spotlight/Nickelodeon, 2001.

Johnston, Marianne. *Let's Visit the Supermarket.* Our Community. New York: PowerKids Press, 2000.

Internet Sites

FactHound offers a safe, fun way to find Internet sites related to this book. All of the sites on FactHound have been researched by our staff.

Here's how:

1. Visit *www.facthound.com*

2. Type in this special code **073682393X** for age-appropriate sites. Or enter a search word related to this book for a more general search.

3. Click on the Fetch It button.

FactHound will fetch the best sites for you!

Index/Word List